Brass Instruments

Music Makers

THE CHILD'S WORLD®, INC.

Brass Instruments

Sharon Sharth

THE CHILD'S WORLD®, INC.

On the cover: These children are playing different types of brass instruments.

Published in the United States of America by The Child's World®, Inc.
PO Box 326
Chanhassen, MN 55317-0326
800-599-READ
www.childsworld.com

Product Manager Mary Berendes
Editor Katherine Stevenson, Ph.D.

Library of Congress Cataloging-in-Publication Data
Sharth, Sharon.
Brass instruments / by Sharon Sharth.
        p. cm.
Includes index.
ISBN 1-56766-985-9 (lib. bdg. : alk. paper)
1. Brass instruments—Juvenile literature.
[1. Brass instruments.]   I. Title.
ML933 .S493 2002
788.9'19—dc21
                              2001005998

Photo Credits
© 1990 Barney Taxel/Mira: 20 (top)
© Bonnie Kamin/Photo Edit: 13
© Chip Henderson/IndexStock: 20 (bottom)
© Corbis Stock Market/Mug Shots, 2003: cover, 2, 6
© Corbis Stock Market/Rob Lewine, 2003: 10
© David Katzenstein/CORBIS: 16
© Franz-Marc Frei/CORBIS: 9
© Philip Gould/CORBIS: 19
© PhotoDisc: 23 (except cornet and sousaphone photos)
© 2001 PhotoSpin: 23 (sousaphone)
© Richard T. Nowitz/CORBIS: 15
© Siede Preis/Getty: 23 (cornet)

Table of Contents

Chapter	Page
Brass Instruments	7
What Are Brass Instruments?	8
How Do You Play a Brass Instrument?	11
What Do Brass Instruments Sound Like?	12
Early Brass Instruments	14
The Trumpet	17
The Trombone	18
French Horns and Tubas	21
Other Brass Instruments	23
Glossary and Index	24

Their music can make you dance and shout. They can sound sad and lonely enough to make you want to cry. You can hear these instruments played alone or in groups. You can hear them in concert halls and dance clubs, and even on the football field! What are they? They're brass instruments!

← This boy is playing a trumpet in a marching band.

What Are Brass Instruments?

Brass instruments are part of a larger group of musical instruments called **wind instruments**. Wind instruments make noise when you blow air into them.

Brass instruments are usually made of a metal called brass. Most of the instrument is a tubelike body. At one end the tube widens into a **bell**. At the other end is a **mouthpiece**, where you place your mouth.

The man on the left is playing a sousaphone. →
The man on the right is playing a trumpet.

How Do You Play a Brass Instrument?

To play a brass instrument, you buzz your lips against the mouthpiece while blowing air into it. Your lips move back and forth quickly, or **vibrate**, against the mouthpiece. The vibrations produce a sound. The air and the sound move through the instrument's body and out the bell.

One way to change the instrument's sound is to tighten or loosen your lips. Your lips become very strong when you play a brass instrument!

← Here you can see how this man holds his lips as he plays a trombone.

What Do Brass Instruments Sound Like?

Brass instruments make many different sounds. Some sound sharp and brassy. Others are gentle and soothing. Some can make all those sounds! Players sometimes use a **mute** to make a brass instrument sound softer and quieter. They stick the mute into the bell or hold it close to the bell's opening.

This trumpet player has put a mute in the bell of his trumpet. →

Early Brass Instruments

Early "brass" instruments weren't actually made of brass. Instead they were made of wood, ivory, or the horns of animals. One of the earliest was the shofar. Ancient Hebrews created this instrument centuries ago. It is still used in Jewish ceremonies today. To play the shofar, you blow air into the smaller end of an antelope's or ram's horn. The shofar plays only two sounds, or **notes**.

This man in Jerusalem, Israel, is blowing ➡ a shofar made from a ram's horn.

The Trumpet

The trumpet is the loudest brass instrument. It has three buttons, or **valves**. The valves push the air in different directions as it moves through the body. Pressing down a valve pushes air into a side tube. The air travels around to the main tube again before going out through the bell. Pressing different valves produces different notes. There is no sound as thrilling as the brassy call of a trumpet!

← These students in Haiti are playing trumpets in a band.

The Trombone

Trombones have a softer sound. They were developed over 600 years ago. Today's trombone is very much like the early ones. It has a mouthpiece and a wide bell. It doesn't have valves like those on a trumpet. Instead it has a long, U-shaped metal **slide**. The slide lengthens or shortens the trombone's tube. Moving the slide in and out changes the notes that are produced.

This young boy is playing a trombone in a café. →

19

French Horns and Tubas

The French horn has a large bell and a narrow tube that coils around many times. It has three valves to change notes. This horn has a soft, gentle sound. It also looks like a fairly small instrument. But if you unroll the tubing, a French horn is over 12 feet long! That's as tall as a man standing on another man's shoulders.

The tuba is one of the biggest brass instruments, and it plays very low notes. It has three or four valves to change the notes. You usually sit down to play the tuba. You rest it on the floor or on your lap and lean it against your body. In a marching band, you carry the tuba and lean it against your shoulder. Tubas come in different sizes, but they're all big and heavy. The largest tuba is 8 feet tall!

← (Top) This girl is showing how to hold a French horn.
(Bottom) This woman rests her tuba on her lap as she plays.

Glossary

bell (BELL)
On a brass instrument, the bell is the wide opening where the air comes out. Different brass instruments have different-sized bells.

mouthpiece (MOWTH-pees)
The mouthpiece is where you put your mouth when you play a brass instrument. To make sounds, you blow air into the mouthpiece while buzzing your lips against it.

mute (MYOOT)
On a brass instrument, a mute is an object you put into or in front of the bell's opening. It blocks the moving air to make the instrument's sound quieter and softer.

notes (NOHTS)
Notes are musical sounds. On brass instruments, you produce different notes by pressing valves or pulling a slide in and out.

slide (SLIDE)
On a trombone, the slide is a movable U-shaped tube that changes the length of the trombone's body. You move the slide in and out to change notes.

valves (VALVZ)
On many brass instruments, valves are buttons you push to produce different notes. The valves change how air flows through the tubelike body.

vibrate (VY-brate)
When something vibrates, it moves back and forth very quickly. Brass instruments produce sound when the player's lips vibrate against the mouthpiece.

wind instruments (WIND IN-struh-ments)
Wind instruments make sound when you blow air into them. Brass instruments are one kind of wind instrument.

Index

Ancient Hebrews, 14

appearance, 8, 17, 18, 21

bell, 8, 11, 12, 17, 18, 21

body, 8, 11, 17

French horn, 21

history, 14

importance, 22

mouthpiece, 8, 11

mute, 12

notes, 14, 17, 18, 21

playing, 8, 11, 12, 14, 17, 18, 21

shofar, 14

slide, 18

sounds, 7, 11, 12, 14, 18, 21

trombone, 18

trumpet, 17

tuba, 21

valves, 17, 21

vibrate, 11

wind instruments, 8